ANIMALS IN THEIR WORLD

Things that POOP in the Night!

Julie K. Lundgren

A Crabtree Seedlings Book

CRABTREE
Publishing Company
www.crabtreebooks.com

Table of Contents

Poop—An EnGROSSing Science! 4

Scat ID 8

Stinky Messages 12

What Goes In, Must Come Out 16

Clean-Up 20

Glossary 23

Index 23

POOP—An EnGROSSing Science!

Scientists study animal poop to learn who lives in an area and what they eat.

The Scoop on Poop!

Other Names for Poop:

- muffins
- pats
- scat
- droppings
- dung
- whitewash
- guano
- castings

Worms, such as earthworms and velvet worms, leave castings.

Nocturnal animals can be hard to find and watch. Their scat gives us clues.

Spotted hyenas hunt at night.

hyena poop

Why Are Some Animals Nocturnal?

Many animals prefer to be awake and active at night because it is cooler. Other animals are active at night to hunt, or to avoid being hunted.

Scat ID

Whose number two? Scientists look at size, shape, and color.

Opossums spend their nights searching for food.

Opossum poop looks like tubes.

Bats and mice leave grains of poop, while bears leave pats the color of their food.

Scientists can test guano (bat poop) to learn what kind of bats live in an area.

In summer and fall, black bear pats are dark from eating berries.

Stinky Messages

Nocturnal animals pass messages in their scat. Some use it to mark their **territories**.

coyote

Coyotes drop scat along the trails that surround their territory.

Male animals find females by smelling droppings.

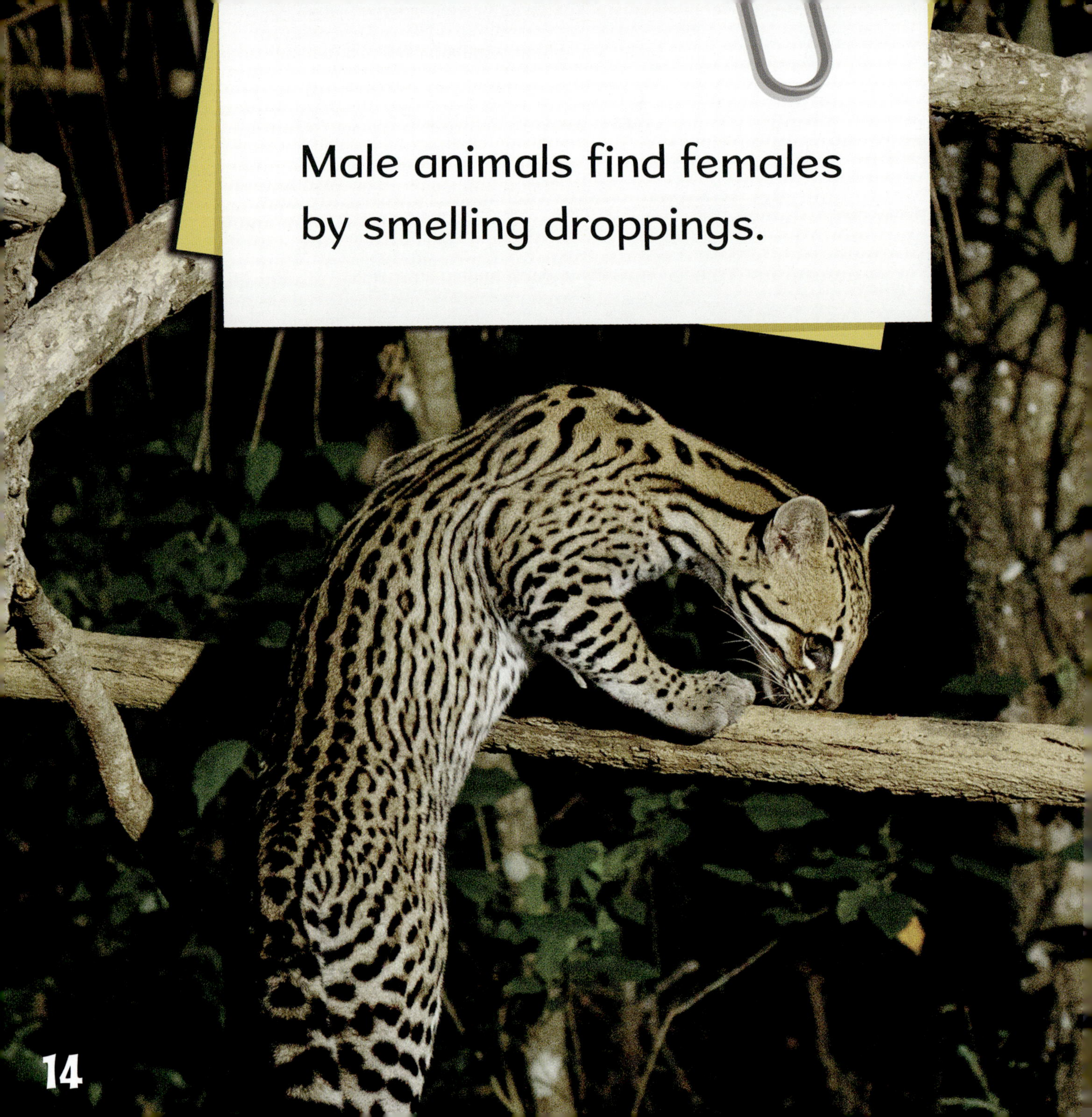

Female ocelots leave stinky valentines for a possible mate.

The Scoop On Poop!

Rabbits, and some other animals, eat their own poop. A second pass through the digestive system captures extra **nutrients**.

What Goes In, Must Come Out

Droppings contain things that animals cannot digest. Seeds and **husks**, peels, hair, bones, and grass may pass through the body.

The cassowary, a nocturnal forest bird, eats fruit and makes seedy dung.

The Scoop On Poop!

Scientists know how to handle animal waste safely. Often, they use gloves and tools. **Microbes** in animal waste can make us sick. Be safe! Look, but never touch.

Tiny microbes cannot be seen without a microscope. Microbes feed on droppings, helping make nutrients and soil for plants.

Mushrooms and other fungi help break down dung piles.

Clean-Up

Animals, wind, and weather **decompose** droppings into soil and food for plants.

The Scoop On Poop!

Dung beetles help clean up droppings by eating them. Some female dung beetles lay their eggs in dung. When the larvae hatch, they eat their "nest"!

When animals eat plants, the **cycle** begins again.

A capybara grazes on large amounts of plants.

Glossary

cycle (SI-kuhl): A natural system that happens over and over in the same order

decompose (dee-kum-POHZ): To cause rot and decay, making the soil rich with nutrients

digestive system (die-JES-tiv SIS-tuhm): A body's process of breaking down food, so it can be used by the body for energy and growth

husks (HUSKS): The outer shell or skin of seeds or plant parts

microbes (MY-krohbz): Very tiny creatures that live in soil, water, or living things. Microbes are part of the food cycle.

nocturnal (nahk-TER-nuhl): Active at night

nutrients (NEW-tree-uhnts): Things needed for healthy growth, such as vitamins and minerals

territories (TAIR-uh-tor-eez): Areas of land that animals defend as their own

Index

bats 10
bears 10
decompose 20
dung beetles 21
mice 10
microbes 18, 19
microscope 19
nocturnal 6, 12
nutrients 15, 19, 22
scientists 4, 8, 18

School-to-Home Support for Caregivers and Teachers

This book helps children grow by letting them practice reading. Here are a few guiding questions to help the reader build his or her comprehension skills. Possible answers appear here in red.

Before Reading

- **What do I think this book is about?** I think this book is about what nocturnal animals do at night. I think this book is about different kinds of animal poop.
- **What do I want to learn about this topic?** I want to learn what nocturnal animals do during the night. I want to learn where nocturnal animals sleep during the daytime.

During Reading

- **I wonder why...** I wonder why scientists study animal poop. I wonder why some animals prefer to be active at night and sleep during the day.
- **What have I learned so far?** I have learned that scientists can test bat poop to learn what kind of bats live in an area. I have learned that animal droppings contain things that animals cannot digest.

After Reading

- **What details did I learn about this topic?** I have learned that dung beetles help clean up droppings by eating them. I have learned that to digest means to break down food, so it can be used by the body for energy and growth.
- **Read the book again and look for the glossary words.** I see the word *decompose* on page 20, and the word *cycle* on page 22. The other glossary words are found on page 23.

Library and Archives Canada Cataloguing in Publication

Available at the Library and Archives Canada

Library of Congress Cataloging-in-Publication Data

Available at the Library of Congress

Crabtree Publishing Company
www.crabtreebooks.com 1–800–387–7650
Print book version produced jointly with Blue Door Education in 2023

Written by: Julie K. Lundgren
Print coordinator: Katherine Berti
Printed in the U.S.A./072022/CG20220201

Photo Credits:

COVER: shutterstock.com | Martin Mecnarowski. Pages 2-3: shutterstock.com | Dirk Ercken. Pages 4-5: istock.com | Ben185, shutterstock.com | Pong Wira, shutterstock.com | Dr Morley Read. Pages 6-7: shutterstock.com | Peter van Dam, shutterstock.com | John Ceulemans. Title page and Page 8: shutterstock.com | IrinaK, page 9: shutterstock.com | Daniella Cortis. Pages 10-11: shutterstock.com | Betty Shelton, shutterstock.com |LifeLoveLiberty. Pages 12-13: shutterstock.com| MelaniWright, shutterstock.com | This servants heart. Pages 14-15: shutterstock.com |PhotocechCZ, shutterstock.com | reisegraf.ch, shutterstock.com | T. M. McCarthy. Pages 16-17: shutterstock.com | MR.PRAWET THADTHIAM, shutterstock.com |slowmotiongli.. Pages 18-19: shutterstock.com | Fat Jackey, istock.com | hekakoskinen. Pages 20-21: shutterstock.com | kram-9, shutterstock.com | Joy Stein, shutterstock.com | Sakdinon Kadchiangsaen. Pages 22-23: shutterstock.com | Leonardo Mercon.

Published in the United States
Crabtree Publishing
347 Fifth Ave.
Suite 1402-145
New York, NY 10016

Published in Canada
Crabtree Publishing
616 Welland Ave.
St. Catharines, Ontario
L2M 5V6